LANDMARK TOP TENS

The World's Most Amazing
Lost Cities

Ann Weil

Raintree

Chicago, Illinois

www.capstonepub.com
Visit our website to find out more information about Heinemann-Raintree books.

To order:
☎ Phone 800-747-4992
🖥 Visit www.capstonepub.com to browse our catalog and order online.

© 2012 Raintree
an imprint of Capstone Global Library, LLC
Chicago, Illinois

Customer Service: 888-454-2279
Visit our website at www.heinemannraintree.com

Edited by Megan Cotugno and Laura Knowles
Designed by Victoria Allen
Picture research by Hannah Taylor and Ruth Blair
Original illustrations © Capstone Global Library Ltd (2011)
Production by Camilla Crask
Originated by Capstone Global Library Ltd
Printed in the United States of America in North Mankato, Minnesota.   062018   000649

Library of Congress Cataloging-in-Publication Data
Weil, Ann.
   The world's most amazing lost cities / Ann Weil.
      p. cm. (Landmark top tens)
   Includes bibliographical references and index.
   ISBN 978-1-4109-4239-5 (hardcover)—ISBN 978-1-4109-4250-0 (pbk.) 1. Extinct cities—Juvenile literature. 2. Cities and towns, Ancient—Juvenile literature. 3. Archaeology—Juvenile literature. 4. Antiquities—Juvenile literature. 5. Civilization, Ancient—Juvenile literature. I. Title.
   CC176.W4 2012
   930—dc22   2010038401

Acknowledgments
The author and publishers are grateful to the following for permission to reproduce copyright material: Alamy Images pp. 4 (© Ruslan Bustamante), 6 (© NASA/Mike Spence), 8 (© Eye Ubiquitous), 27 (© Mary Evans Picture Library); Bridgeman Art Library p. 7 (© Look and Learn); Corbis p. 20 (Richard A Cooke); © Edison Caetano p. 25; Getty Images pp. 16 (Philippe Bourseiller), 21 (David H Collier); Mary Evans Picture Library p. 5; Photolibrary pp. 12 (Photononstop/Frederic Soreau), 14 (JTB Photo), 23 (Robert Harding Travel/Christian Kober), 26; Shutterstock pp. 9 (© kated), 10 (© ethylalkohol), 11 (© Alexey Stiop), 15 (© mg1408), 17 (© David Wardhaugh), 18 (© Hu Xiao Fang), 19 (© mathom), 22 (© OPIS).

Cover photograph of Machu Picchu, Peru, reproduced with permission of Shutterstock (© Bryan Busovicki).

We would like to thank Daniel Block for his invaluable help in the preparation of this book.

Every effort has been made to contact copyright holders of material reproduced in this book. Any omissions will be rectified in subsequent printings if notice is given to the publisher.

Contents

Lost Cities 4

Atlantis 6

Pompeii 8

Machu Picchu 10

Ubar 12

Troy 14

Borobudur 16

Angkor 18

The Pueblos of Chaco Canyon..20

Petra 22

El Dorado 24

The Lost City of Z 26

Lost Cities Facts and Figures 28

Glossary 30

Find Out More 31

Index 32

Some words are printed in bold, **like this**. You can find out what they mean in the glossary.

Lost Cities

How have cities become lost? Sometimes people abandoned a city for unknown reasons. Some ancient cities were destroyed by natural disasters. Rungholt, a city on a German island, sank into the ocean during a terrible storm in 1362.

Lost and found

Some lost cities are found by accident. Others are found by people who believe in the legends of lost cities. In the past, those looking for lost cities risked their lives going long distances through dangerous places. Today new technology helps people look for and find lost cities without leaving home.

Ruins of the great **Aztec** city of Tenochtitlán were found buried under Mexico City.

Lost or Fiction?

Some "lost cities" may never have existed at all. Poems and stories tell of magical kingdoms, such as Avalon and Camelot, which feature in the legends about King Arthur. Some people believe the legends are true. But no one has yet proved that King Arthur really existed.

This is an artist's version of how Camelot may have looked.

Atlantis

One of the oldest legends of a lost city comes from Ancient Greece. The Greek **philosopher** Plato (c. 427–347 BCE) wrote about an island he called "Atlantis." He described it as a kind of **paradise** that sank into the ocean. Was Atlantis just another of this great thinker's ideas? Or did the place really exist?

Atlantis

Location: Near the Straits of Gibraltar, Western Europe

That's Amazing!
An ancient text describes Atlantis as a great civilization with 10 kingdoms.

Some people believe Plato's Atlantis was on this Greek island, now called Santorini.

This is an artist's idea of how the destruction of Atlantis might have looked.

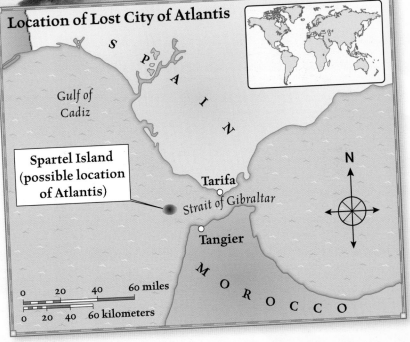

Location of Lost City of Atlantis

SPAIN

Gulf of Cadiz

Spartel Island (possible location of Atlantis)

Tarifa

Strait of Gibraltar

Tangier

MOROCCO

N

0   20   40   60 miles

0   20   40   60 kilometers

In fact there is a sunken island in the same area that Plato described. In 2001 a French scientist put forward the idea that Spartel Island in the Gulf of Cadiz had inspired the legend of Atlantis. Experts believe it is possible that an earthquake and **tsunami** destroyed this island about 12,000 years ago. But so far there is no proof that a great ancient **civilization** existed there, and the search for Atlantis continues.

Pompeii

This ancient city in Italy was once a thriving **port** and **resort** town for wealthy Romans. No one knew that the nearby mountain was really a sleeping volcano on the verge of waking up. The deadly eruption happened in 79 CE. The entire town was buried under 20 feet (6 meters) of volcanic ash.

Pompeii

Location: Near the city of Naples, Italy

That's Amazing!

The same volcano that buried Pompeii has erupted many times since. Another deadly eruption in 1631 killed more than 3,000 people.

Mount Vesuvius is still active today. It is the only active volcano on the mainland of Europe.

A forgotten city

More than 1,000 years passed and people forgot about this once great city. It was rediscovered in 1748. Today, Pompeii is a window into life during the **Roman Empire**. Some of the city was almost perfectly preserved under the layers of volcanic ash. Also preserved were the bodies of people killed by poisonous gases from the volcano. Body casts show them lying as they fell in the streets nearly 2,000 years ago.

Lava hardened around the dead bodies, preserving their shape long after the flesh had rotted away.

Machu Picchu

In 1911 an American explorer named Hiram Bingham was searching for the lost **Inca** city of Vilcabamba in Peru. A guide led him up into the Andes Mountains. He showed Bingham a lost Inca city. But it wasn't the one he was looking for. This was a bigger, even more amazing Inca city—Machu Picchu!

There are around 140 structures at Machu Picchu.

Protected by Steep Cliffs

Machu Picchu is surrounded by 1,500 foot- (450 meter-) high cliffs on three sides. A steep mountain towers behind it. It is very hard to get to! This may be why it stayed hidden from much of the world for so long.

The stones at Machu Picchu fitted together so well that no cement was needed to hold them in place.

Machu Picchu
Location: Peru, South America
That's Amazing!
Archaeologists think Machu Picchu may have been a vacation home for Inca kings!

Lost city of the Incas

Machu Picchu was built around 1450. It was abandoned less than 100 years later. The people there may have died of **smallpox**. This deadly disease came from Europe with Spanish **conquerors** hoping to find gold in the New World. But Machu Picchu was never **looted** by the conquerors.

Ubar

Arabian legends describe a great city called Ubar. This city was a trading center for **frankincense**, a kind of incense made from dried tree sap. Frankincense was very valuable in the ancient world. Stories say Ubar vanished around 300 CE. Its exact location was forgotten. Explorers searched for it in the Rub al-Khali desert. But no one could find it.

Ubar

Location: Ancient Arabia (present-day Oman)

That's Amazing!
Ubar is known as the Atlantis of the Sands, because it was buried beneath the desert sand dunes.

Scientists are slowly rebuilding the jumbled ruins of Ubar.

Using modern tools to find Ubar

In 1992 explorers used modern technology to track down the lost city. It was buried beneath sand dunes in the southern desert. Photos taken from a space shuttle showed ancient paths through the desert that were almost impossible to spot from the ground. **Radar** was used to see through the sand that covered the ancient buildings. The radar images and photographs showed **archaeologists** where to start digging.

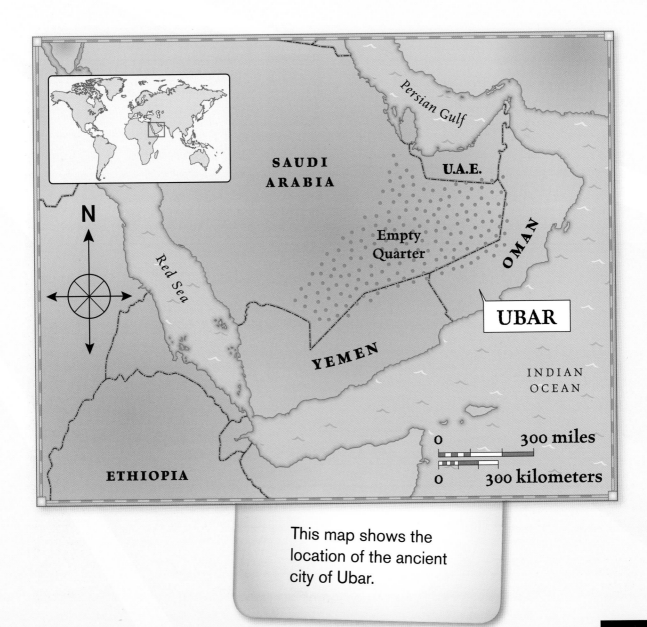

This map shows the location of the ancient city of Ubar.

Troy

The *Iliad* is an Ancient Greek **epic** poem set in and around the city of Troy. For a long time no one knew whether Troy had really existed. Then in 1871 an explorer found ruins matching the description of Troy. As he dug deeper he discovered layers of older and older buildings. Eventually he uncovered nine cities! Each new city had been built on the ruins of the old one.

Troy
Location: Northwestern Turkey
That's Amazing!
Most **archaeologists** thought Troy was just a **myth** until it was discovered in 1871.

The first city of Troy was built around 3000 BCE. The last one dates from about 100 CE.

This Trojan Horse was made for the 2004 Hollywood movie *Troy*. It is now on display in Turkey, near the site of ancient Troy.

The Trojan Horse

The people of Troy were called Trojans. They fought a war with the Greeks. A legend tells how the Greeks tricked the Trojans so they could get inside their walled city. The Greeks built a huge wooden horse and left it at the city gates. Thirty soldiers hid inside the hollow horse. The rest of the Greek army pretended to sail away. The Trojans thought the war was over. They brought the horse into the city. That night, the hidden Greeks crept out and opened the gates for their army.

Borobudur

At some point during the 14th century, the **Buddhist** site of Borobudur on the island of Java in Indonesia was abandoned. For centuries it lay hidden by thick layers of volcanic ash and jungle. Then in 1814 it was rediscovered by a team of explorers led by Sir Thomas Raffles from Britain. The team quickly realized that they had uncovered the largest Buddhist temple in the world!

Carvings written in an ancient language called Sanskrit convinced experts that Borobudur was built between 750 and 850 CE. The site was an important place of Buddhist pilgrimage. The design of the temple is a guide to the teachings of the Buddha. Visitors begin at the first level and walk up. Each new level represents a higher step of enlightenment.

Borobudur
Location: Island of Java, Indonesia
That's Amazing!
Borobudur has the largest Buddhist temple in the world.

Nobody knows for certain why Borobudur was abandoned, but it is possible that volcanic eruptions drove people away.

The Buddha

Buddhism is a major world religion. It began in India more than 2,500 years ago. A prince named Siddhartha Gautama left his palace and family to live a simple life. He became known as "the Buddha." Over many years, Buddhism spread from India to other places in Asia and then throughout the world. Most people in Indonesia today are **Muslim**, but there is still a Buddhist minority living there.

There are hundreds of Buddha statues on and around the temple.

Angkor

Angkor in Cambodia was the capital of a powerful kingdom in Southeast Asia from about 800 to 1400 CE. This ancient city was home to up to 1 million people! Satellite photos show that roads and **canals** extend over an area as big as the city of Los Angeles.

Angkor
Location: Cambodia, Southeast Asia
That's Amazing!
At one time, Angkor was the largest city in the world!

Angkor was declared a **World Heritage Site** in 1992.

Angkor Now

For many years, wars in Cambodia kept tourists away from Angkor. But today Angkor is busy with tourists again. Few visit all the temples in Angkor. There are more than 1,000! The largest is called Angkor Wat. It was built as a temple where **Hindu** people could worship.

The five central towers of Angkor Wat represent the five peaks of Mount Meru, the **mythical** home of the Hindu gods.

What happened then?

Angkor was abandoned sometime in the 1400s. Without written records from that time, it is impossible to know for sure what really happened. Perhaps the city was invaded or ran out of water.

The Pueblos of Chaco Canyon

Chaco Canyon in New Mexico is dry, stony land. It is extremely hot in summer and freezing cold in winter. Despite its harsh climate Chaco Canyon was once the center of a highly developed Native American culture. Ancient people built large **pueblos** connected by more than 400 miles of roads.

The Pueblos of Chaco Canyon

Location: New Mexico, USA

That's Amazing!
Some of the ancient roads from Chaco Canyon were up to 40 feet (12 meters) wide!

Some of the pueblos were five stories tall, with large rooms and high ceilings.

Round rooms called *kivas* were built for religious ceremonies. The biggest *kivas* could hold around 400 people.

More mysteries

There are no written records to tell us how many people lived there. Some experts think around 5,000 people lived in a total of 400 communities. Some time around 1200 CE, the Chacoans abandoned their pueblos in the canyon. Perhaps the lack of water during a **drought** finally drove the people away. But until there is new evidence, we may never know the whole truth about these mysterious people.

Petra

In 1812 a Swiss explorer was traveling from Syria to Egypt. He had heard rumors of ancient **relics** in a hidden valley. At that time it was dangerous for Europeans to travel in Arabia. The explorer disguised himself as an Arab so he would not stand out. He was the first European to enter this hidden city for 700 years.

Petra
Location: Jordan, the Middle East
That's Amazing!
The only entrance to the city of Petra is a narrow crack in the natural rock walls.

Known as the Treasury, this building was probably a royal **tomb** or temple.

This building is called the Monastery, but it was probably a temple. Its nickname might have come from the crosses carved inside.

Lost city of stone

Petra was built by an ancient **civilization** called the Nabataeans. The word *Petra* means "rock." This amazing city of temples, tombs, and houses was carved out of sandstone cliffs! This ancient city was a center for the spice trade. It was also famous for its complicated waterworks. There were dams to control **flash floods** and conserve water. Visitors can still see remains of the pipes, waterways, and **reservoirs** that the people of Petra used more than 2,000 years ago!

El Dorado

Spanish **conquerors** thought people in Central and South America were hiding their gold in secret cities. The story of El Dorado told of a king whose body was covered in gold. This part of the story may have been true! Legends tell of a **ritual** where a king was sprayed with tiny bits of gold after his body was painted with something sticky. Then he sailed out into the middle of a lake and jumped into the water!

This map shows the possible location of the lost city of El Dorado.

Finally found?

The Spanish never found their city of gold. Explorers searching for the city died in the Amazon rain forest. Now experts may be able to finally find El Dorado. Photographs of areas where the rain forest has been cleared were taken from the air. These show geometric shapes on the ground. Experts think this could be the location of an ancient civilization. If this is true, then this lost city may be found at last.

Experts believe that these marks were left by an ancient settlement. Was this once the legendary city of El Dorado?

El Dorado

Location: Somewhere in the Amazon rain forest, South America

That's Amazing!
Logging in the rain forest has made it easier to find the lost city of El Dorado.

The Lost City of Z

Fans flock to watch movies about adventurers searching for lost cities. Some of these fantastic stories are based on facts. A Portuguese explorer who lived in the 1700s wrote about his visit to a city that might have been the legendary El Dorado. He described what he saw there, but he did not give its exact location. This document was preserved in a library in Rio de Janeiro, Brazil.

The rain forest was a dangerous place, with ferocious animals, deadly snakes, and hostile tribes that attacked with poisoned arrows.

Many people thought Percy Fawcett was crazy. Few believed that a civilization could have existed in such a harsh place.

A real-life Indiana Jones

In the early 1900s a British man named Percy Fawcett traveled to Brazil. He was determined to find this lost civilization, which he called the City of Z. He had many adventures in the Amazon jungle before he disappeared in 1925. Most people assume that Fawcett died in his quest for this lost city.

Lost Cities Facts and Figures

There may be many lost cities still waiting to be discovered. The latest technology gives explorers new tools they can use to find them without leaving their computers. So the search for lost cities continues. Which lost city do you think is the most amazing?

Atlantis
Location: Near the Straits of Gibraltar, Western Europe

That's Amazing!
An ancient text describes Atlantis as a great **civilization** with 10 kingdoms.

Pompeii
Location: Near the city of Naples, Italy

That's Amazing!
The same volcano that buried Pompeii has erupted many times since. Another deadly eruption in 1631 killed more than 3,000 people.

Machu Picchu
Location: Peru, South America

That's Amazing!
Archaeologists think Machu Picchu may have been a vacation home for **Inca** kings!

Ubar
Location: Ancient Arabia (present-day Oman)

That's Amazing!
Ubar is known as the Atlantis of the Sands, because it was buried beneath the desert sand dunes.

Troy
Location: Northwestern Turkey
That's Amazing!
Most archaeologists thought Troy was just a **myth** until it was discovered in 1871.

Borobudur
Location: Island of Java, Indonesia
That's Amazing!
Borobudur has the largest **Buddhist** temple in the world.

Angkor
Location: Cambodia, Southeast Asia
That's Amazing!
At one time, Angkor was the largest city in the world!

The Pueblos of Chaco Canyon
Location: New Mexico, USA
That's Amazing!
Some of the ancient roads from Chaco Canyon were up to 40 feet (12 meters) wide!

Petra
Location: Jordan, the Middle East
That's Amazing!
The only entrance to the city of Petra is a narrow crack in the natural rock walls.

El Dorado
Location: Somewhere in the Amazon rain forest, South America
That's Amazing!
Logging in the rain forest has made it easier to find the lost city of El Dorado.

Glossary

archaeologist someone who studies ancient remains

Aztec ancient civilization that lived in the region that is now Mexico

Buddhism ancient religion that follows the teachings of Buddha

canals human-made waterways

civilization group of people with a highly developed culture and way of life

conqueror person who has defeated others and taken their land

drought water shortage caused by a lack of rain

epic long poem that tells an exciting story and usually celebrates a great hero

frankincense kind of incense made from the sap of a desert tree that was very valuable in the ancient world

flash flood sudden rush of water after heavy rain

Hindu person who follows the Indian religion of Hinduism

Inca ancient civilization that lived in the region that is now Central America, Peru, and Ecuador

looted stolen

Muslim person who follows the religion of Islam

myth story or legend, often not based on fact

paradise perfect place

philosopher thinker who seeks wisdom by trying to understand and explain the nature of life and what is real

population number of people living in a specific area

port town along a river or near the ocean where ships can be loaded and unloaded

pueblo settlement of high-rise stone or adobe houses; Spanish for "town"

radar machine that uses radio waves to find or track faraway objects

relic ancient object

reservoir lake of water that forms behind a dam

resort place that people go to for a vacation

ritual set of actions, usually performed for religious reasons

Roman Empire large area including much of Europe controlled by an ancient civilization (27 BCE – 395 CE) based in Rome, Italy

smallpox disease that can spread quickly and easily to many people. Many Native Americans died from this disease, which causes a high fever and a blister-like rash.

tsunami huge wave caused by an earthquake

tomb grave, cave, or other place where a dead body is buried

World Heritage Site place with outstanding historical value

Books

Linnéa, Sharon. *Mysteries Unwrapped: Lost Civilizations*. New York, NY: Sterling, 2009.

Newman, Sandra. *The Inca Empire.* New York, NY: Children's Press, 2010.

Stern, Steven L. *Wretched Ruins*. New York, NY: Bearport, 2010.

Walker, Kathryn. *The Mystery of Atlantis*. New York, NY: Crabtree, 2010.

Websites

http://www.factmonster.com/spot/atlantis1.html
Is the city of Atlantis just a myth? Find out more on this website.

http://www.harcourtschool.com/activity/pompeii/index.html
Go on a virtual tour of Pompeii, and find out what happened on the fateful day when Mount Vesuvius erupted!

Amazon rain forest 24–27
Angkor 18–19
archaeologists 13, 14
Atlantis 6–7
Aztecs 4

Bingham, Hiram 10
Borobudur 16–17
Buddhism 16, 17

Cambodia 18–19
Camelot 5
canals 18
Chaco Canyon 20–21

deserts 12, 13
drought 21

earthquakes 7
El Dorado 24–25, 26

Fawcett, Percy 27
flash floods 23
frankincense 12

Hinduism 19

Iliad 14
Incas 10
Indonesia 16–17
Italy 8–9

Jordan 22–23

King Arthur 5
kivas 21

legends 4, 5, 15, 24

Machu Picchu 10–11
Mount Meru 19
Mount Vesuvius 8

Native Americans 20–21
New Mexico 20–21

Oman 12–13

paradise 6
Peru 10–11
Petra 22–23
Plato 6
Pompei 8–9
pueblos 20–21

radar 13
religious ceremonies 21
Roman Empire 8, 9
Rungholt 4

Sanskrit 16
Santorini 6
smallpox 11
Spanish conquerors 11, 24

temples 16, 17, 19, 22, 23
Tenochtitlan 4
trade 12, 23
Trojan Horse 15
Troy 14–15
tsunamis 7
Turkey 14–15

Ubar 12–13

Vilcabamba 10
volcanoes 8, 9, 16

World Heritage Sites 18